quaranta giorni

forty days

Paula Martin

EARTH SONGS PRESS
A Division of Sacred Flow Arts
www.sacredflowarts.com

Earth Songs Press

QUARANTA GIORNI: FORTY DAYS

Cover Artwork:
"Contemplation" by Rhonda Danette Owen

Printed in the United States of America
ISBN 978-0-578-48075-6

Forty days and forty nights
You were fasting in the wild;
Forty days and forty nights,
Tempted, and yet undefiled.

~George Hunt Smyttan (1856)

contents

introduction

quarantine (n.)
Italian quarantena, from Venetian dialectal Italian, quarantine of a ship (so called because the length of the quarantine was typically forty days), from Old Italian quarantina, period of forty days (such as one designated for fasting or penance), quaranta giorni, literally "space of forty days," from quaranta, forty, from Latin quadrāgintā; see kwetwer- in Indo-European roots.

[American Heritage Dictionary of the English Language, 5th ed.]

March 22, 2020, nine days into a fever that would last another seven days, I sat down at my desk, turned on my phone, and recorded myself reading my poem "Woman" (written six months before) to post to Facebook. I don't remember what drove me to do something so completely out of character as posting a video of myself; it must have been a combination of the fever, the isolation, and the collective stress from pandemic that was just beginning to spread worldwide. In any case, that one recording turned into a daily ritual of intuitively choosing a previously written poem, recording it, and then sharing it. I didn't think about how long I would be doing this, or what, if anything, I would end up doing with the collection of poems now forming. All I knew was that it was helping me tremendously to focus my day around an aspect of introspection. And maybe, just maybe, it was helping someone else.

It wasn't until the thirty-eighth poem on the thirty-eighth day that I realized that there was an end in sight. While I had heard of Jesus's forty days in the desert, Rumi's forty days in the cave, and Noah's forty days in the boat (among other forty-day transformative stories), it hadn't occurred to me until day thirty-eight that I was on a forty-day healing journey. And then I realized that not only was I doing it individually, but we were all on a forty-day healing journey collectively: *quarantine* is derived from the Italian *quaranta giorni*, "forty days." It couldn't get any more obvious than that.

Whether we were wandering in a desert, silent in a dark cave, or floating aimlessly on endless water, we were all being given the opportunity to go inward. Worldwide. Chosen for us, not by us. Whether we chose to resist or take the opportunity to heal was up to us.

This collection is my forty days in the same order that I shared them from March 22 – May 01, 2020. Because the poems were chosen each morning, they in many ways capture the journey of isolation while reminding us how to find hope, beauty, and connection even as the world as we know it is stripped away.

I have included a section in the back that breaks the poems down into themes. If you are led to intentionally strike out on your own forty-day journey, there are many ways to use this book as a guide. You can go in the order that I did, or you can intuitively choose a poem for any given day and let that guide you. You can choose a theme for the day or week, or you can choose different poems at different times of the day to see what may be guiding you at that moment. You can write your own poems, create your own art, sing your own songs. Whatever resonates for you is exactly what you need.

We each go on our own forty-day journeys multiple times throughout our lifetimes. The opportunity to heal is always there, whether we are quarantined or free, recognize it or not. It's a never-ending cycle. With the spring 2020 pandemic quarantine, we were forced to slow down. But we can slow down and go inward any time to reflect and learn and heal. We can start the journey any time.

Ultimately the question is what we do once we walk out of the desert, emerge out of the cave, step onto dry land. Do we take up our ministry, become mystics, create new worlds? Or do we try to recreate what was before (but can never be again), no matter how broken it may have been? Either way, we're all in this together.

This is big work we're doing, my friends. And big work is being done to and through us. See you out there, in here, and on the other side.

~Paula, 2020

Woman

She rations her love
like Depression-era sugar—
half a teaspoon here,
a pinch there—
while we sit on our hands
mouths open like baby birds.
If she would only remember
her love can't be bought or stolen,
that the more she gives
the more she creates,
like two fish in a basket,
five loaves of bread—
maybe then she would realize
that no matter what they tell her
she still carries the power
to turn spirit to matter,
water to wine,
and that She is the Savior
we have been waiting for
all along.

Salvation

I close my eyes and descend
into my darkness, once again
to mine for deposits
I've mistaken for sin

chipping away at mountains,
digging in thick, red clay,
feeling blindly along the walls
of dank, dark caves

until my fingers graze an edge
100 miles underground
and in the darkness I taste freedom
on my tongue like a sound

so I dig and I pull
my hands shaking, heart racing
until it loosens, then releases
from its lifetime of casing

then I turn and I stumble
with the weight of the stone,

catch my breath, regain my footing,
make my way back home

to the surface, to the light
as the stone begins to sing
rainbow prisms of forgiveness—
and I open my wings.

Love Letter

I left you a love letter
taped to the moon,
words I've spent a lifetime
scribbling in sand,
brushing on autumn leaves,
singing river stones smooth.
I'm told if I just keep
sending them out they will find
you— the same words
sung in silence by the temple priest,
whispered in the dark
by the pharaoh's daughter,
reflected in the eyes of the slave.
Maybe tonight's the night
they will be carried across oceans,
then tomorrow rise into clouds to fall
on your cheek in a drop of rain—
and time will stop
as you look up, remember, and know.
Like a long-forgotten kiss.
Like the memory of snow.

What I Know: I

The stone on your windowsill
sings medicine songs while you sleep,

the oak in your yard
encircles your whole house with light,

the river you drive over
carries your shame effortlessly downstream,

the mountain in the distance
prays for you in an ancient tongue,

and the moon outside your window, who's been
patiently waiting your whole life for you to remember,

cradles your dreams against her milky-white breast,
your story in the palm of her hand.

Avra Kadavra

I see words peering out
from your forced, weary smile,
magic words, if set free
can change water to wine

but you keep your lips tight
tend to silence, to pain,
not knowing it's light, not sin
you contain.

One day they may tire,
slip out and take flight,
cast spells of creation
reflecting the light—

but for now they take peeks
at the freedom beyond,
the rest of your life balanced
on the tip of your tongue.

Truth

She flows
into rooms
like a river
unannounced
lapping walls
soaking floors
in spirals and swirls
overtaking all dams
she then roars around doors
fills my lungs—drowning—breathless—

until I let go
and float.

What I Know: IV

The stones that you hid as a child
still wait for you in mossy tree stumps,

the fairies still hold your secrets
in the palms of their hands,

the baby bird's bones still dream peacefully
under the roots of the old oak,

the creek still sings the songs
of the stars.

And your imaginary friend,
who has watched you every day
through a stranger's eyes,

still curls up beside you as you close your eyes,
white wings covering you as you sleep.

Love Story

I held my love
in the palm of my hand,
my worthiness slipping through my fingers
like a fistful of sand

as I longed for connection,
proof I wasn't alone,
like a child aching for a mother
who's staring at her phone

yet the more the wind blew
and scattered the grains
the less words had meaning
until only silence remained

and in the silence I discovered,
empty-handed and alone,
the vast ocean of my worth
lapping at the shore.

Uncut

At fifty I've decided to let my hair
grow free and wild, no longer tamed
by society's standards, uncolored
and uncut to my hips,

a trail of silver strands
marking my presence in places
they should no longer linger—

shut in car doors, sat on in church,
floating unseen on the back
of a young man's shirt
like a lover.

Scheherazade

We think the stories that we tell
keep us alive
night after night, 1000 tales,
spun by firelight

caves of gold, magic words,
carpets that fly,
relying on our wit and our wisdom
to barely survive

until the 1001st dawn
when we wake up alone
out of stories, no more words,
bare to the bone

and we finally realize
the way to be free—
so we step inside, own our story,
and transform into Queen.

What I Know: XII

If only for a moment
you can close your eyes and trust,

allow your past to slip unbuckled
to a puddle at your feet

the wind will whisper like a lover
in the language of the stars

and you'll remember you are weightless, free—
a gentle, rolling sea.

The Vision

The man my 11-year-old son will become
surfaced on his face today,
eyes deep in thought, jaw set.

I stopped breathing.
I missed my chance to say goodbye.

Then, as soon as he appeared
he was gone, boyhood
returning in deep dimples,
mischievous laughter
running out the backdoor
as I exhaled.

Maybe one day he will attempt
to carry the weight of the world
on his back, or discover
how to change lead to gold,
water to wine
and I will search to find
the boy within the man,
eyes wide with wonder.

But for now he jumps on the trampoline

and tries to grab clouds, his hands

soft and round like a secret,

like a dream.

Learning to Listen

What if our grandmothers sing to us
in the falling leaves,
the soar of the bird,
the morning dew,

the woodpecker's knock
on a Georgia pine,
the eyes of a stranger,
rain.

What I Know: X

The wind longs to share
your dreams with the moon,

the mountain yearns to hold your secrets
in the center of her chest,

the river pines to carry
your prayers to the sea,

and the fire, who waits patiently at the edge
of every moment,

aches to kiss you with the heat
of a thousand suns

then take your hand
and dance.

Free

The older I get
the more I long to be
carried by the wind—
free from the past,
empty of regret,
willowy and white
like a feather,
like the lean in
for a first kiss.

Lost Language

There are secrets buried deep
in my daughter's hair,
her thick, black curls
hiding the forgotten words
of a curandera, a chief, a slave.

Sometimes I hear them,
my fingers freeing them as I braid,
and they stir, wake up,
rise unexpectedly through time.

I wonder what messages they bring
we can no longer understand.

What I Know: VI

Long-forgotten dreams
lay sleeping in your bones,
lifetimes of promises
buried deep like stones

but they are not yours to carry
over and over through time
and if you can just set them down
I promise you will find

your grandmothers' prayers etched
in the palms of your hands
longing daily to show you
the promised land

and the secrets of the stars
you thought were out of reach
waiting patiently in each breath
for you to remember—and sing.

North Star

When women remember
the secret songs of the moon,
the ancient poems in our blood,
our sacred contract to dream

we'll rise up like stars
to the inky black sky,
light the way like a compass,
a prophecy, a prayer.

Beloved

I think I glimpsed you once
in a lonely man's eyes
like the glint on a sword
of a mountain sunrise,
like a ray of light
through a crack in a door
lighting shards of glass
into stars on the floor.

I think I heard you once
in a whisper at dawn
like the hum of light
of a distant star,
like the echo of rain
in a morning mist
rising gently and softly
to the edge of a kiss.

I think I tasted you once
on warm, salty skin
like the foam of the sea
brushing the shore once again,

like the memory of snow
in the middle of June
as crystalline on my tongue
as a kiss from the moon.

I think I smelled you once
in dark tousled hair
like woodsy secrets of trees
not meant to share,
like ancient promises whispered
spiced and sweet in the dark
riding thin lines of smoke
curling up to the stars.

I think I felt you once
on a lying man's lips
like velvety waves on the surface
of sinking ships,
like the world opening up
where the river meets the sea
weightless and floating
expansive and free.

I know I loved you once
over and over again

like the sun breaks the dawn

and new life begins,

like déjà vu

each lifetime disguised

as the next line of a poem

in a newborn's eyes.

What I Know: XIII

When the first light of day
begins to glow with allow
and you're still floating, weightless,
between then and now

if you can wait there, suspended
no expecting, no need,
your six-year-old self
will awaken and see

the echo of dreams
in the earth's gentle mist,
your great-grandmother's prayers
on the shimmering grass

and the words of the bird
in his rising sun song
and you'll remember you're loved—
and you've been all along.

Grace

I groan as change rolls in
on fast-moving clouds,
her presence announced with a clap,
the silence of birds.

I jump down from the swing
run fast for the door,
pressure falling, tension rising,
and brace for the storm.

Rain pelts on the glass
as I push the door shut
safe inside, hunkered down,
metal sliding in wood.

Then the trees catch my eye,
heads bowed, bodies swaying,
roots deep, arms waving
hallelujah in prayer.

Second Sight

I long to see
the secrets of trees,
the songs of stones,
the stories of stars,
yesterday's prayers in a rainstorm,
tomorrow soaring on wings—

like a soothsayer, a seer,
a mystic,
a poem.

Infinity

If I show up in this moment
empty-handed, palms up

could you be brave enough
to fill the space between us
with only breath?

What I Know: XI

If you relax your hearing,
let your thoughts slip
away like silk,
the birthsongs of stars
will echo back to you—

like the inky blackness
of a newborn's eyes,
like a prayer.

Medicine Song

What if our mother sings us to life
with each rising sun,
our bones soft with dreams,
stardust shimmering on skin,
her song older than time
sung by her mountains, her stones,
gently coaxing us to awaken,
to remember, to hear.

What I Know: III

You shine with the light
of a thousand stars—
like a firefly on a summer night,
like a poem.

Naming

I've kept a lifetime of secrets
of truth unexpressed,
words I didn't dare utter
held tight in my chest

hoping someday they'd soften
lose their color, their shape,
like an old pair of jeans
or a memory with age

and eventually unravel,
just letters, no sin,
scatter north, south, east, west
faded threads in the wind

but no matter my effort
to deny they exist
their wholeness lingers in my breath
like a shadow, a mist

so tonight I will own them
speak their names, set them free

to soar to the gods
on Mercury's wings.

If you could

hear me in the glisten
of yesterday's rain,

smell me in the yellow
of falling leaves,

touch me in the sweetness
of a ripe pear,

taste me in the songs
of faraway stars—

could you then maybe,
just maybe,

see you in me?

Teacher

I wonder if my grandmother's magnolia
remembers my breath,
the swirl of my fingertips,
the salt of my tears,

if she's waited forty-five years
for me to come home,
crawl into her shadows,
curl up in her arms

the child she taught how to sit
among waxy green leaves
close my eyes, hold my breath
and listen to stars.

What I Know: VIII

In the pause between breaths,
suspended in time and space
your Self waits to show you
what it's been trying to your whole life—
that there's no need to prove, no need
to compete, no need to impress—
and if you can just let go,
relax into the respite and believe,
the demand to know, to do, to be
will fall down like stardust,
like rain.

Reflection

What if it's possible
that every person you meet today
loves you without question—

no matter what they say
no matter what they do—

and their whole job
is to reflect back to you
what you think you are hiding
in the palm of your hand—

like the face of a mountain
on a crystal blue lake,
like God.

Autumn

What if the trees you drive by daily
know your secrets as their own

hold your dreams in buried roots
store your pain in hardened knots

sing you love songs as you sleep
leave you poems on dying leaves

blazing reds, yellows, oranges
crunching unheard underfoot.

Invitation

Tonight at 3am,
under the cover of stars,
close your eyes
and meet me
in the exquisite darkness,
in the pause between breaths,
where truth is no longer
bound by facts
and flows like a river,
like a song.

Absolution

I loved you once, in silence,
as the moon loves the sun,
caught in an endless loop of longing
for a touch that will not come.

And you loved me, too, in silence,
though you've chosen to forget.
So terrified of your shadow.
Of being wrong. Of regret.

So you spend your days pretending,
creating stories as you shine,
my name suspended in your breath
balanced carefully in your fire.

And I spend my nights confessing,
shifting words from dark to light.
Freeing us both from ancient covenants
that have bound us throughout time.

What I Know: V

If you sit quietly enough,
allow the silence to dissolve
your thoughts to dust
and breathe in and out
with the rhythm of the stars,

words will soar in unannounced,
their wings damp with the dew
of a thousand dreams,
light gently on the page

and sing.

Equinox

I woke up this morning
the sky burning with orange
the air empty around me—
my story was gone.

A lifetime of words
repeated thousands of times
were suddenly absent, no trace,
disappeared in the night.

In the cover of darkness
in the depth of my dreams
they must have flittered, then fluttered,
flown into the flames.

Now the oak's dying leaves
reflect the heat of the sun
and autumn's medicine song sits perched
on the tip of my tongue.

Trust

I long to sit
in a seer's silence—
unquestioning, unflinching,
fully accepting like an oak
tucked tightly into an acorn,
like a prophet.

What I Know: IX

Every time you risk it all
to be seen, really seen

a tiny crack spreads across
my shell from inside—

tap-tap-tapping
to be set free

and fly.

Revelation

I woke up this morning
weary-boned and quiet
to discover that after
a lifetime of searching
I have been here all along—
lingering in the shadows
of half-told truths,
peering out from behind
the words of a poem,
dissolving like sugar
on the tip of a lover's tongue—
my true breadth and depth,
not visible to the naked eye,
patiently waiting, waiting, waiting
beneath rolling blue waves
to be remembered—
like a mountain rising
thirty-three thousand feet
from the ocean's floor,
like God.

Star Song

I sent a poem out to find you
in the black moonless night
each word carrying a universe,
a galaxy,
a star

in the hopes that you'll recognize
in the vast open spaces
the whisper of eternity
and in the echo
your song.

themes

acknowledgments

The following poems first appeared in these books (Earth Songs Press):

North Star: "Woman," "Love Letter," "Truth," "Scheherazade," "Learning to Listen," "Lost Language," "North Star," "Grace," "Second Sight," "Medicine Song," "Teacher," "Reflection," "Autumn," "Equinox," "Revelation."

What I Know: "What I Know: I," "What I Know: II," "What I Know: III," "What I Know: IV," "What I Know: V," "What I Know: VI," "What I Know: VIII," "What I Know: IX," "What I Know: X," "What I Know: XII," "What I Know: XIII."

Croning: "Uncut," "Free," "Infinity," "If you could," "Invitation," "Trust."

about the poet

Paula Martin is a writer, teacher, and healer who has been helping people tap into their own divine essence for over 25 years.

about the artist

Rhonda Danette Owen is a writer, editor, artist, and former journalist in Little Rock, Arkansas. She lives with her husband, Michael Foster, and their tenacious terrier, Heidi.

www.ingramcontent.com/pod-product-compliance
Lightning Source LLC
Chambersburg PA
CBHW040057100426
42734CB00035B/79